Edition Schott

Clarinet Library · Klarinetten-Bibliothek

Carl Maria von Weber
1786 – 1826

Variationen über ein Thema aus der Oper „Silvana"

Variations on a theme from the opera "Silvana"

für Klarinette (in B) und Klavier
for Clarinet (in B♭) and Piano

opus 33

Nach dem Text der Carl-Maria-von-Weber-Gesamtausgabe herausgegeben von
Edited from Carl Maria von Weber, Complete Works by
Joachim Veit

KLB 59
ISMN 979-0-001-14096-6

SCHOTT

www.schott-music.com

Mainz · London · Berlin · Madrid · New York · Paris · Prague · Tokyo · Toronto
© 2005 SCHOTT MUSIC GmbH & Co. KG, Mainz · Printed in Germany

Vorwort

Zur Entstehung des Werkes

Die *Silvana*-Varitionen schrieb Weber auf der gemeinsamen Konzertreise mit dem Klarinettisten der Münchener Hofkapelle, Heinrich Joseph Baermann, für einen Auftritt in Prager Adelshäusern. In seinem Tagebuch notierte er am 14. Dezember 1811 in Prag „Früh die *Variat:[ionen]* über das *Thema* aus *Silvana* für *Clar:[inette]* und *Fortep:[iano] componirt"*, und noch am selben Abend erlebte das Werk im Hause des Reichsgrafen Karl Anton Firmian (1770 – 1822) und dessen Ehefrau Maria Anna, geb. Gräfin Althann (1775 – 1840) im Palais Kinsky seine Uraufführung. Weber hatte offensichtlich die Hoffnung, mit diesen Variationen über ein Thema aus seiner 1810 vollendeten dreiaktigen Oper *Silvana* das Prager Publikum auf dieses Werk aufmerksam zu machen. Wenige Tage später verhandelte Weber erfolgreich mit dem Prager Theaterdirektor Liebich über den Verkauf des *Abu Hassan* und der *Silvana*.

Die kurze Variationsreihe über das *Silvana*-Thema (in dem zugehörigen Textabschnitt aus der Szene und Arie der Mechthilde „Warum mußt ich dich je erblicken, o Philip, in der Waffen Glanz" beklagt Mechthilde das Schicksal, das sie zu dieser verbotenen Liebe geführt hat) gehörte dann auf der weiteren Konzertreise mit Baermann zu den häufig musizierten Stücken der beiden Künstler (u. a. am 18. Dezember 1811 in Prag, am 24. und 25. Januar 1812 in Gotha, am 30. Januar und 2. Februar in Weimar, am 14. Februar in Dresden und am 12. März in Berlin). Weber selbst schrieb am 31. Dezember 1811 an seinen Freund Gotttfried Weber: „*componirt* habe ich seit München nichts als in Prag *Variat:* für *Bärmann* und mich die nicht schlecht sind".

Bei dem recht eilig komponierten Werk griff Weber auf den Kopfsatz der Nr. 5 seiner bereits im Herbst 1810 in Darmstadt komponierten *Six Sonates progressives pour le Pianoforte avec Violon obligé* op. 10 (II), zurück, der aus dem auf 16 Takte erweiterten *Silvana*-Thema und vier sich anschließenden Variationen besteht, von denen Weber drei in op. 33 übernommen hat: So entsprechen sich die beiden ersten sowie die letzte Variation (inclusive Coda) beider Werke (zu den Einzelheiten vgl. Serie VI, Bd. 3 der Gesamtausgabe). Mit op. 33 kehrte Weber aber zur ursprünglichen Besetzung des Opernthemas mit Soloklarinette zurück, verwendete nun aber statt der A- eine B-Klarinette, schob nach der II. Variation drei weitere ein und ersetzte die in der Mollvariante erklingende ursprüngliche *Marcia*-Variation von op. 10/5 durch ein *Lento*, das nur noch Rudimente dieser Vorlage aufweist.

Die Quellen des Werkes

Die Quellenlage zu den Variationen ist äußerst dürftig, denn alle authentischen handschriftlichen Quellen sind verloren. Dies ist umso beklagenswerter als in diesem Falle ungewöhnlich zahlreiche Zeugnisse aus erster Hand existierten: Weber hatte zwei unabhängig voneinander niedergeschriebene Autographe hinterlassen, da er das Werk im September 1812 in Weimar/ Gotha offensichtlich nicht mitführte und für die Weimarer Großherzogin Maria Pawlowna neu aufschreiben musste, die dann bei einer Aufführung am 27. Oktober selbst den Klavierpart übernahm. Auch von der Kopie, die Weber in diesem Zusammenhang der Großherzogin überreichte, ließ sich keine Spur mehr finden, ebensowenig von der sicherlich von ihm kontrollierten Kopistenabschrift, die im Februar 1814 in Prag als Stichvorlage für den Schlesingerschen Druck entstand. Auch in Baermanns Besitz blieb offensichtlich nichts erhalten, ebenso ist eine Abschrift aus dem Besitz Giacomo Meyerbeers seit 1945 verschollen. So musste als nahezu einzige authentische Quelle der bei Schlesinger im April 1814 mit der Plattennummer „108" erschienene Stimmen-Erstdruck dienen. Eine Ausnahme bilden lediglich die Hinweise auf das 1812 entstandene zweite Autograph, die sich in einem Berliner Exemplar der bei Schlesinger Anfang 1854 erschienenen Klavierpartitur mit Solostimme (Plattennummer „S. 108") fanden, in dem F. W. Jähns nach der Einsichtnahme in das damals noch erhaltene Autograph 2 etliche Abweichungen vermerkte. Nur insofern als die dabei von Jähns bezeichneten Details auch für die publizierte Fassung zwingend sind, wurden sie vom Herausgeber im edierten Text (in gekennzeichneter Form) berücksichtigt, weitere Eigenheiten sind im Revisionsbericht der WeGA dokumentiert. Im übrigen gibt es zum Erstdruck als Hauptquelle für eine Edition des Werkes keine Alternative, was umso bedauerlicher ist, als die Stecher Schlesingers die Weberschen Vorlagen erfahrungsgemäß meist eher unzuverlässig wiedergaben.

Zu Heinrich Joseph Baermanns Anteil an der Komposition und zur Ausgabe seines Sohnes Carl

Baermanns Sohn Carl hat in einem Brief vom Oktober 1864 an den Weber-Forscher Friedrich Wilhelm Jähns geäußert, diese Variationen seien „von Weber & Vater eigentlich zusammen *componirt"* worden und führt weiter aus, dass „namentlich die 3t *Variat:[ion] Adagio* von Vater *componirt* ist. So viel ich mich aus Vaters Erzählung klar erinnere, hätten Sie daßelbe in einer Nacht in Prag den Tag vor einer größeren Gesellschaft *componirt* u. Tags darauf daselbst gespielt".

Es erscheint in der Tat denkbar, dass die III. Variation, in der das Klavier eine rein harmonisch-stützende Begleitfunktion hat und die Ausdrucksfähigkeit der Klarinette im gesamten Klangspektrum im Vordergrund steht, nicht nur vom Spiel Baermanns inspiriert ist, sondern auch in der Substanz auf dessen Vorschläge zurückgeht.

In einem weiteren Brief vom 3. Januar 1863 spitzte Baermann seine Darstellung noch zu, indem er behauptete: „Doch weiß kein Mensch wie diese *Variation (: Adagio :)* eigentlich gespielt wird als ich, da Vater dieselbe ganz anders spielte, als sie im Drucke erschienen ist [...]". Schließlich schreibt er vier Jahre später anläßlich der bevorstehenden Publikation seiner Neuausgabe sämtlicher Klarinettenwerke Webers bei Lienau/Schlesinger, dass die Solostimme dieser Variation, so wie sie gedruckt stünde, „eigentlich nur den Anhaltspunkt für den *Clavierspieler* gegeben" habe: „Ich habe nun alle diese Stellen auf das Genaueste so gegeben wie sie von Vater mit Weber gespielt wurden". Schon an einem solchen Punkt zeigt sich die Problematik der Behauptungen Baermanns: Von einer Drucklegung der Variationen bereits in einem sehr frühen Stadium kann keine Rede sein – Weber hatte das Werk vor der Anfertigung einer Stichvorlage bereits zahlreiche Male mit Baermann zusammen aufgeführt und da zwischen seiner Niederschrift und der späteren Prager Druckvorlage offensichtlich nur geringe Unterschiede bestehen (wie sich bei der Analyse der Quellen zeigt), hätte die „spätere Geschmacksausbildung" Webers, von der Baermann in diesem Zusammenhang spricht, kaum Spuren hinterlassen.

Die Aussage Carl Baermanns hat außerdem zu einer Fehldeutung der Wiedergabe dieser III. Variation geführt. Die alternative Fassung, die in Baermanns Edition unter dem Haupttext der Klarinettenstimme abgedruckt ist (und die häufig auf die Wiederholungen bezogen wird), ist in den genannten Briefen nicht ausdrücklich als jene bezeichnet, die von seinem Vater stamme (vielmehr galt das ja für die Variation als solche). Allenfalls könnte dieses *Ossia* eine Erinnerung an Heinrich Baermanns Interpretationen dieser Variation sein. Viel eher aber handelt es sich hier um eine Form der Auszierung des Vorgegebenen, wie sie in Carl Baermanns eigenen Werken üblich ist. In der Rezeption der Baermann-Edition setzte sich aber bald missverständlich eine falsche Gegenüberstellung dieser „Heinrich-Baermannschen" Fassung und der darüber abgedruckten Weberschen „Originalfassung" durch. Übersehen wurde dabei auch, dass schon die Auftakte, die sich in dieser Fassung finden, keineswegs aus der Vorlage stammen, sondern erst von Carl Baermann eingefügt wurden, ebenso wie etliche Vorschriften zum Tempo, zur Dynamik oder zur Artikulation, die den Angaben des auf Weber zurückgehenden Erstdrucks widersprechen.

Dennoch blieb die Baermann-Ausgabe bis in die jüngste Zeit die maßgebliche Richtschnur aller folgenden Editionen (vgl. hierzu ebenfalls WeGA Serie VI/3, S. 125ff.).

Zur vorliegenden Edition und zu einigen Notationsbesonderheiten Webers

Die vorliegende, mit dem Notentext der Carl-Maria-von-Weber-Gesamtausgabe übereinstimmende Edition folgt dem kritisch durchgesehenen Erstdruck. Alle Ergänzungen in runden Klammern entsprechen Details des verlorenen zweiten Autographs, die durch Jähns' Einträge im Berliner Exemplar der späteren Ausgabe des Werkes dokumentiert sind. Vom Herausgeber zwingend für notwendig befundene weitere Zusätze stehen in eckigen Klammern. Die Notation folgt so eng wie möglich der Vorlage, ggf. aus Gründen der besseren Lesbarkeit notwendige Eingriffe sind im Revisionsbericht der WeGA verzeichnet. Ausdrücklich sei nochmals darauf hingewiesen, dass auf jegliche nicht eindeutig bestimmbare Ergänzungen verzichtet wurde, wodurch einerseits die Defizite der Quellen deutlicher dokumentiert werden, andererseits aber auch Einschränkungen der Interpretationsfreiheit vermieden werden können.

Erheblicher Spielraum bleibt vor allem bei der Ausgestaltung der **Dynamik**, die – bereits mit dem Thema beginnend – nur sehr lückenhaft vorgeschrieben ist (vgl. auch T. 12-14). Um nur zwei Beispiele zu nennen: Kehrt die Themenwiederholung in T. 13 der I. Variation zum *dolce* des Anfangs zurück? Bleibt sie im *pianissimo* oder soll sie *piano* erklingen? Ist die Hervorhebung in T. 15 als bewusster Kontrast auf die rechte Hand des Klaviers beschränkt? Angesichts der vielfältigen klanglichen Differenzierungen in Webers Musiksprache sollte auf vorschnelle Angleichungen verzichtet werden.

Bögen und Artikulationszeichen sind in der Hauptquelle oft uneinheitlich gesetzt; gleichartige Takte können dennoch meist ohne Skrupel in der jeweils zuvor angegebenen Art weiter bezeichnet werden (z.B. die Bögen zu den Triolenfiguren der Variation VII, vielleicht mit Ausnahme von T. 9/10). Zu beachten ist, dass Bögen oft zur Bezeichnung eines *sempre legato* dienen und dann in ihrer Ausdehnung frei wechseln (vgl. z. B. im Thema T. 1-2 mit 9-10 rH oder Variation III, T. 1-4 mit 5-8 rH), ohne dass artikulatorische Einschnitte gemeint sind. **Akzente** sind in ihrer Ausdehnung vereinzelt unklar, könnten also teils auch als lange *decrescendi* verstanden werden (z. B. Var. IV, T. 11-12; zu Einzelheiten vgl. Revisionsbericht zu Bd. VI/3).

Die **Tempoangabe** lautet in dem übernommenen Abschnitt der Nr. 10 der *Silvana Andantino*, in der Sonate op. 10/5 dagegen *Andante con moto*, was sich nach Jähns wohl auch im Autograph 2 fand. Probleme ergeben sich auch bei der Taktvorzeichnung. Im zweiten Autograph war laut Jähns bereits im Thema ein *alla-breve*-Zeichen notiert (so auch in op. 10/5, nicht jedoch im entsprechenden Abschnitt der *Silvana*-Partitur), ebenso in allen Variationen außer Nr. VI.

Das Verzierungszeichen in T. 4 des Themas ist als Trillerzeichen lesbar (so auch in der *Silvana* und in op. 10/5). Im Erstdruck ist vor T. 9 des Themas ein doppelter Taktstrich mit **Wiederholungszeichen** in beide Richtungen eingetragen, am Ende von T. 18 jedoch lediglich ein gewöhnlicher Taktstrich in der Klarinette und dünne doppelte Taktstriche im Klavier; die Endtaktstriche in T. 20 haben keine Wiederholungszeichen. Im Autograph 2 fehlten nach Angabe von Jähns die beiden Takte 19-20, am Ende von T. 18 standen offensichtlich Wiederholungszeichen und zusätzlich eine Fermate über und unter dem Taktstrich des Klaviers. In der Sonate op. 10/5 sind im Autograph und Erstdruck Wiederholungstaktstriche für beide Teile eingetragen. Die Wiederholung des zweiten Teils (wie sie in den folgenden Variationen stets bezeichnet ist) müsste nach T. 18 beginnen, so dass die T. 19-20 als Anhang zu betrachten sind.

In Variation I war laut Jähns im Autograph 2 in T. 2 die **Artikulation** an das Klavier bzw. an T. 14 angepasst. Als *staccato*-Zeichen werden im Erstdruck lediglich Striche verwendet; dies gilt auch für die Bezeichnung der *portati*, während der spätere Druck hier differenziert. Da Jähns hierzu nichts anmerkt, ist anzunehmen, dass auch das Autograph 2 beide Formen unterschied, so dass der Herausgeber in diesen Fällen Punkte übernahm. Keine eindeutigen Hinweise geben die Quellen zur Ergänzung von **Vorschlägen** in dieser Variation, während in Variation V zumindest in T. 1, 5 und 15 eine Ergänzung der Vorschläge in der Klarinette nahezuliegen scheint, obwohl auch hier alle drei Takte in der Klarinette nur zur ersten Note einen Vorschlag notieren.

Die *Tempo-Primo*-Vorschrift zur IV. Variation bezieht sich auf die Wiederaufnahme des Grundtempos bzw. des Tempos der ersten Klavier-Solo-Variation II. Diese ist auch in der Sonate op. 10/5 mit einer schnellen Tempovorschrift (*Vivace*) versehen.

In Variation VI gibt Weber die Art der Auflösung der *tremolando*-Bezeichnung im Klavier nicht an. In Variation VII dürfte die Kombination der Viertelnoten mit Strich in T. 2-4 der linken Hand als Variante der Notierung von Achtelnoten mit Pause zu verstehen sein. Andererseits haben aber auch die in T. 1 mit Pausen notierten Noten der linken Hand bereits Striche zur Bezeichnung des *ben marcato*, so dass die Notationsweise hier unlogisch oder zumindest zweideutig erscheint.

Ein herzliches Wort des Dankes gilt an dieser Stelle allen Bibliotheken und Personen, die zur Entstehung der vorliegenden Ausgabe beigetragen haben. Für alle weiteren Einzelheiten zu dem Werk, seiner Entstehung, Überlieferung und Edition sei auf den Band der Gesamtausgabe verwiesen.

Joachim Veit

Preface

Genesis of the work

Weber composed the Variations on a theme from *Silvana* on a concert tour undertaken jointly with Heinrich Joseph Baermann, the clarinettist in the Munich court orchestra; they were intended for performance in the homes of the aristocracy in Prague. He noted in his diary on 14 December 1811 in Prague: "morning, *composed* the *Variat.* in *B flat* on a *theme* from *Silvana* for *Clar:*[inet] and *Fortep:*[iano]", and the work was given its first performance that same evening in the Kinsky Palace, the residence of the Imperial Count Karl Anton Firmian (1770 – 1822) and his wife Maria Anna, née Countess Althann (1775 –1840). Weber was evidently trying to generate interest in Prague for his three-act opera *Silvana*, which he had completed in 1810, with these variations on a theme from the work. A few days later Weber successfully negotiated the purchase of *Abu Hassan* and *Silvana* with Liebich, director of the Prague theatre.

The theme from *Silvana* comes from a scene and aria sung by Mechthilde, "Why did I ever have to see thee, O Philip, in the battle's glow?", where Mechthilde laments the fate that has led her to this forbidden love; the short series of variations was to be one of the pieces most often played by Weber and Baermann on the rest of their concert tour (including performances on 18 December 1811 in Prague, on 24 and 25 January 1812 in Gotha, on 30 January and 2 February in Weimar, on 14 February in Dresden and on 12 March in Berlin). Weber himself wrote in a letter to his friend Gottfried Weber on 31 December 1811: "Since Munich I have *composed* nothing, except, in Prague, *Variat.* for *Bärmann* and myself, which are not bad."

The work was composed in a great hurry and Weber made use of the first movement of No. 5 from the *Six Sonates progressives pour le Pianoforte avec Violon obligé* Op. 10 (II), which he had composed in Darmstadt in the autumn of 1810. This consisted of the *Silvana* theme extended to sixteen bars and four subsequent variations, of which Weber used three again in Op. 33: the first two variations and the last one (including the coda) in the two works thus correspond (for further details see Series VI, Vol. 3 of the complete edition). In the Variations, Op. 33 Weber returned to the original instrumentation of the opera theme with solo clarinet, but now using a B♭ clarinet instead of a clarinet in A. He added three more variations after Variation II and replaced the original *Marcia* variation in the tonic minor with a *Lento* that retained only rudiments of its predecessor.

Sources for the work

The available source documents for the Variations are scant indeed, since all the authenticated manuscript scores have been lost. This is all the more regrettable as in this instance we have an unusually large number of first hand accounts of the existence of these manuscripts. Weber left two independently written autograph scores: he evidently did not take the work with him to Weimar/Gotha in September 1812 and had to write it out again for the Grand Duchess of Weimar, Maria Pavlovna, who then played the piano part herself for a performance on 27 October. No trace remains of the copy Weber gave to the Grand Duchess on that occasion, nor of the engraver's copy made in Prague in February 1814 by a copyist and presumably checked by Weber himself when the work was published by Schlesinger. It is clear that no score remained in Baermann's possession, while another copy belonging to Giacomo Meyerbeer has been lost since 1945. The first edition of the parts published by Schlesinger in April 1814 with the plate number "108" has therefore had to serve as almost the only authentic source. Our only other source of information is references to the second autograph manuscript of 1812 made in a Berlin copy of the piano score with solo part (plate number "S. 108") published by Schlesinger at the beginning of 1854, in which F. W. Jähns noted a number of discrepancies after examining the second autograph score, which was then still in existence. Only where the details identified by Jähns offer imperative improvements on the published version have they been adopted by the editor (with their provenance identified) for inclusion in this score; details of individual instances are given in the editorial report in the WeGA. Otherwise there is no alternative to using the first edition as the main source text for a new edition of the work, which is all the more regrettable as it has been found that Schlesinger's engravers often made rather unreliable reproductions of Weber's original notation.

Heinrich Joseph Baermann's role in the composition and the edition by his son Carl

Baermann's son Carl stated in a letter written in October 1864 to the Weber researcher Friedrich Wilhelm Jähns that these variations were "in fact jointly *composed* by Weber and Father" and went on to say that "indeed the 3rd *Variat.: Adagio* was *composed* by Father. From what I can clearly recall of what Father said, they *composed* it in one night in Prague on the eve of a large social gathering and played it the very next day."

Indeed it is quite conceivable that Variation III, in which the piano provides a purely harmonic supporting accompaniment, yielding centre stage to the expressive qualities of the clarinet across its whole tonal spectrum, was not only inspired by Baermann's playing, but may have been substantially based upon his suggestions.

In another letter dated 3 January 1863 Baermann pointed his remarks further by asserting: "Yet no one other than myself knows how this *Variation (: Adagio :)* is actually to be played, since Father played it quite differently from the way it is printed [...]". Then four years later, in a letter written *à propos* the forthcoming publication of his new edition of Weber's complete clarinet works by Lienau/Schlesinger, Baermann says that the solo part in this variation as it is printed "served merely as a guide to the *pianist*. I have now reproduced all these passages exactly as they were played by father with Weber". This quotation, however, illustrates the problem with Baermann's claims. There can be no suggestion that the *Silvana* Variations went to print at a very early stage: Weber had already performed the work with Baermann numerous times before an engraver's copy was ever made, and as only minor differences can be found between his transcript and the printer's copy subsequently used in Prague (as will be seen by analysing these scores) the 'later evolution of his taste' mentioned by Baermann in this connection would seem to have left few traces.

Carl Baermann's comments have also led to a misinterpretation of the way in which this Variation III is presented on the page. The alternative version that is printed below the main body of the clarinet part in Baermann's edition (and which is often used for repeats) is not explicitly described in the letters mentioned as that composed by his father (this claim rather applies to the variation itself). At most, this *Ossia* might be a recollection of Heinrich Baermann's interpretation of this variation. It is far more likely, however, that it is a form of ornamentation of the given version, as is commonly found in Carl Baermann's own works. The way the Baermann edition was received, however, soon led to an erroneous opposition between the "Heinrich Baermann" version and Weber's "original version" printed above it. Meanwhile the fact was also overlooked that the upbeats with which this version begins do not come from the original score but were added by Carl Baermann, as were a number of indications of tempo, dynamics and phrasing which contradict the instructions given by Weber in the first printed edition. The Baermann edition was nevertheless considered until very recently as establishing the guidelines for all later editions (again, see WeGA Series VI/3, pp. 125ff.).

The present edition and some of the idiosyncrasies of Weber's notation

This edition, which matches the score in the complete edition of Carl Maria von Weber's works, is based on a critical revision of the first edition. All additions in round brackets correspond to details from the lost second autograph manuscript, documented by Jähns' entries in a Berlin copy of the later edition of the work. Further additions felt by the editor to be necessary are put in square brackets. The notation follows the original as closely as possible; where changes have been made for the sake of improved legibility, these are detailed in the WeGA editorial report. It should be pointed out again that no details have been added which could not be clearly authenticated; on the one hand this has facilitated clearer documentation of any deficiencies in the sources used, and on the other hand we avoid putting constraints on freedom of interpretation.

Plenty of room for interpretation is left in particular by the placing of **dynamic markings**, which – even with the opening theme – leaves many gaps (see also bars 12-14). To cite just two examples: does the recapitulation of the theme in bar 13 of Variation I return to the *dolce* of the beginning? Does it remain *pianissimo* or should it sound *piano*? Should only the notes in the right hand be brought out in bar 15 to create a deliberate contrast? In view of the many differentiated sounds that make up Weber's musical language we should beware of being too keen to make one bar match another.

Slurs and phrase marks are often very inconsistently placed in the main source edition; bars that are similar can usually be marked in the manner previously indicated (e.g. slurs over the triplet figures in Variation VII, perhaps with the exception of bars 9/10). It should be noted that slurs are often used to indicate *sempre legato* and then the length of slurs may vary (compare for example bars 1-2 in the theme with the r.h. in bars 9-10 or, in Variation III, bars 1-4 with the r.h. in bars 5-8), without implying a break in the phrasing. In some instances it is not clear how far **accents** are to be applied; some of them may be understood as long *decrescendi* (e.g. Var. IV, bars 11-12; for details see editorial report for Vol. VI/3).

The **tempo indication** in the section taken from No. 10 in *Silvana* is *Andantino*, whereas in the Sonata Op. 10/5 it is given as *Andante con moto*, which according to Jähns probably also appeared in the second autograph manuscript. Problems also arise with **time signatures**.

In the second autograph score, according to Jähns, there was an *alla breve* time signature for the theme (as in Op. 10/5, but not in the corresponding section of the *Silvana* score) and all the Variations apart from No. VI. The ornament marked in bar 4 of the theme can be read as a trill sign (as in *Silvana* and in Op. 10/5). In the first edition there is a double barline with **repeat signs** in both directions before bar 9 of the theme, whereas at the end of bar 18 there is just an ordinary barline in the clarinet part and thin double barlines in the piano part; the final barlines in bar 20 do not have repeat signs. In the second autograph manuscript Jähns tells us that the two bars 19-20 were missing, and that there were repeat signs at the end of bar 18 with a fermata above and below the barline in the piano part. In the Sonata Op. 10/5 there are repeat signs at the barlines for both sections in the autograph score and in the first edition too. The repetition of the second section (as always indicated in the following variations) should begin after bar 18, so that bars 19-20 are to be regarded as an appendix.

According to Jähns, in the second autograph manuscript the **articulation** in bar 2 of Variation I matched that in the piano part and in bar 14. In the first edition only vertical strokes were used as *staccato* markings; this also applies to the marking for *portati*, while the later printed version differentiates between the two. As Jähns does not comment on this we can assume that the second autograph manuscript also distinguished between the two styles, so the editor has used dots in these instances. The sources used give no clear guidance as to the way **grace notes** are to be played in this variation, while in Variation V at least in bars 1, 5 and 15 it seems more natural to write out the ornaments in the clarinet part, although here too all three bars only give a grace note before the first note in the clarinet part.

The *tempo primo* marking at the beginning of Variation IV relates to a return to the underlying tempo, or to the tempo of the first piano solo Variation II. This also happens in the Sonata Op. 10/5, where a fast tempo marking *(Vivace)* is given.

In Variation VI Weber does not indicate how the *tremolando* marking in the piano part is to be interpreted. In Variation VII the combination of crotchets with lines in bars 2-4 in the l.h. may be understood as a variant of the notation of quavers with a pause. On the other hand, though, the notes in the l.h. in bar 1 marked with pauses already have lines to indicate *ben marcato*, so that the manner of notation here seems illogical or at least ambiguous.

Sincere thanks are due at this point to all the libraries and people who have contributed to the preparation of this edition. For any further details relating to the work, its genesis, provenance and editorial history, reference should be made to the relevant volume of the complete edition.

Joachim Veit
Translation Julia Rushworth

Silvana-Variationen op. 33

Carl Maria von Weber
1786–1826
(WeV P. 7)

Andante con moto

*) Zur Taktangabe vgl. Vorwort; keine Angabe zur Dynamik.
**) Im Autograph 2 stand hier laut Jähns als Variante der rH:

Var. I

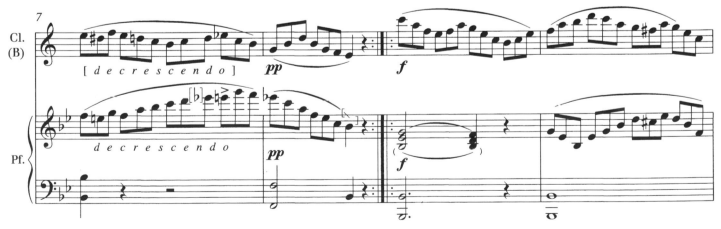

*) Zur Wiederholung des zweiten Teils vgl. Vorwort.
**) Zu den Vorschlägen in Cl und Pf vgl. Vorwort.
***) Zur Artikulation vgl. Vorwort.

Schott Music, Mainz 52 027

*) Im Autograph 2 in T. 11 < > und lediglich *f* notiert.
**) Im Autograph 2 laut Jähns *crescendo* bis zum *ff*.

Clarinetto in B♭

*) Im Autograph 2 möglicherweise in erster Takthälfte *crescendo* notiert.
**) Im Erstdruck ab Zählzeit 2 jeweils keine Vorschläge notiert (vgl. auch T. 15).
***) Im Autograph 2 möglicherweise ganztaktig *crescendo* notiert.

Clarinetto in B♭

Silvana-Variationen op. 33

Carl Maria von Weber
1786–1826
(WeV P. 7)

*) Zur Taktangabe vgl. Vorwort; keine Angabe zur Dynamik.
**) Zur Wiederholung des zweiten Teils vgl. Vorwort.
***) Zur Artikulation vgl. Vorwort.
****) In den Quellen keine Angabe zur Dynamik.

© 2005 Schott Music GmbH & Co. KG, Mainz   Printed in Germany   KLB 59

*) In den Quellen keine Angabe zur Dynamik.
**) Im Autograph 2 laut Jähns in der rH als Variante:

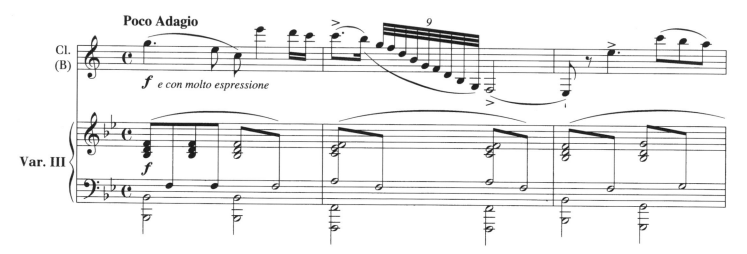

Tempo Primo
Animato e con fuoco

*) Im Autograph 2 vermutlich Arpeggier-Symbol notiert.

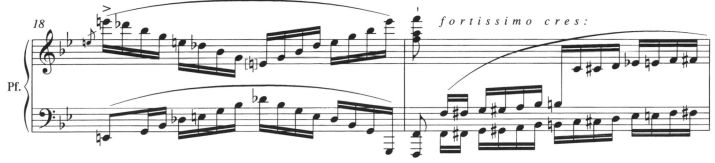

Var. V

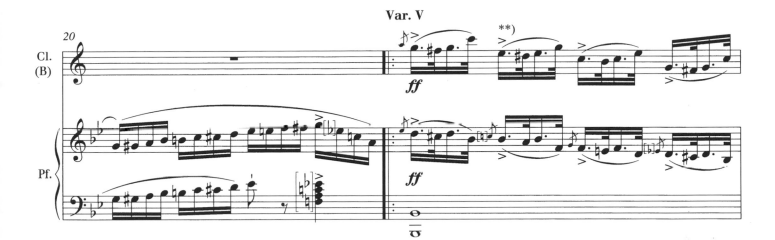

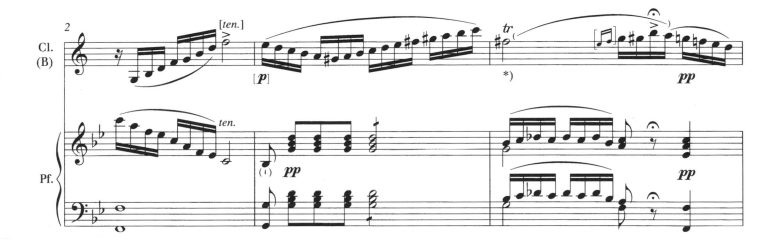

*) Im Autograph 2 war möglicherweise in der ersten Hälfte von T. 4 ein *crescendo* notiert.

**) Im Erstdruck sind weiterhin in der Klarinette ab Zählzeit 2 keine Vorschläge notiert, aber vermutlich zu ergänzen (vgl. auch T. 15).

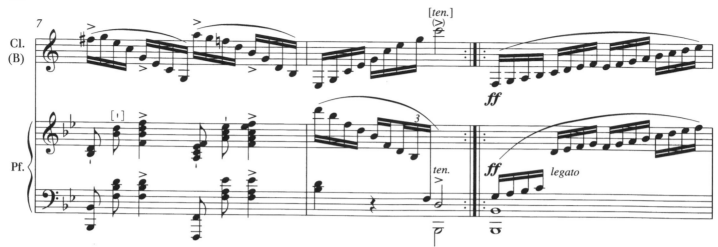

*) Im Autograph 2 möglicherweise ganztaktig *crescendo*.

2222222222

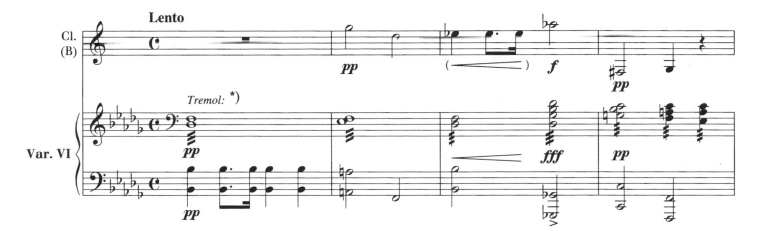

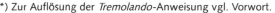

*) Zur Auflösung der *Tremolando*-Anweisung vgl. Vorwort.
**) Im Autograph 2 möglicherweise in T. 9 *f* zwischen den Systemen des Pf; in T. 11 der Kl ◁▷ sowie lediglich *ff* notiert.

*) Im Autograph 2 laut Jähns *crescendo* bis zum *ff*.

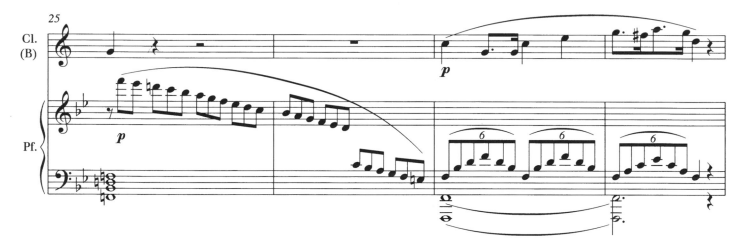

Fine